Celebrate
Thanksgiving

Deborah Heiligman
Consultant, Dr. Elizabeth Pleck

NATIONAL GEOGRAPHIC
WASHINGTON, D.C.

family

A Texas farmer and his
son harvest soybeans.

turkey

In Autumn, when fields are full and crops are ready, people all over the world give thanks for the harvest.

In the United States, on the last Thursday in November, we celebrate Thanksgiving.

We celebrate with turkey, family, and counting blessings.

> *A wild turkey in Florida*

counting blessings

We hear about what we call the "first Thanksgiving." In 1621, new English settlers in Plymouth, Massachusetts, celebrated a good harvest. They had survived a difficult year with the help of the Wampanoag Indians who lived there already.

The Wampanoag had been having festivals of thanks for many years. So when they heard the English celebrating, they killed five deer and brought them to the harvest festival to share.

∧ *At a reenactment at Plimoth Plantation, English settlers welcome Wampanoag Indians to their celebration.*

We hear about the "first Thanksgiving."

< *A cornucopia of squash, vegetables, and nuts*

> *Felicity Duran performs Thanksgiving songs with her classmates in Hobbs, New Mexico.*

They feasted on venison, roast duck, geese, clams, lobster, oysters, fish, Indian corn, dried berries, and stewed pumpkin. We don't know for sure if they ate wild turkey. We know they did not have cranberry sauce, potatoes, pumpkin pie, or apple pie. All of that came later.

For three days the 52 Pilgrims (as they came to be called) and 90 Indians played games and sports, sang, and danced. And they feasted!

< A Wampanoag feasts at Plimoth Plantation.

They feasted.

< A man throws two hatchets at the Thanksgiving Festival at Berkeley Plantation. The event marks the Thanksgiving day held in Virginia in 1619, which was actually the first Thanksgiving observed by English settlers in America.

v Dogs eat, too, at Plimoth.

The history of what happened between European settlers and Native Americans in our country is a sad one. In Plymouth, a few years after the feast there was a war between the settlers and the Indians. Many of the Wampanoag were killed. All over our country there were battles, and the Native Americans were forced from their land. Today some Indians mourn on Thanksgiving. Others feast on turkey and cranberry sauce with their families. Still others have special ceremonies of thanks, as they have done for thousands of years.

Some Indians mourn;

∧ Andres Araica prays at the statue of Massasoit in Plymouth, Massachusetts, on the annual Day of Mourning, held on Thanksgiving.

< Ashley Matt does a shawl dance during a Native American Thanksgiving meal served to elementary school children in Kalispell, Montana.

some have ceremonies of thanks.

9

> Every year the President of the United States grants an official pardon to a turkey, who is then allowed to live the rest of its life on a farm—instead of ending up as someone's Thanksgiving dinner.

After the feast in 1621,

Thanksgiving was not a regular celebration. We owe Thanksgiving as we know it today to a writer and editor named Sarah Josepha Hale. Sarah Josepha Hale thought all Americans should celebrate Thanksgiving day at the same time every year. She wrote to every President for more than twenty years. Finally, Abraham Lincoln declared a national day of Thanksgiving in 1863. Now every year we all celebrate on the same day.

> This is the Thanksgiving proclamation that President Lincoln issued on October 2, 1863. It created a national Thanksgiving holiday.

HAPPY THANKSGIVIN

We all celebrate
on the same day.

We travel
miles and miles.

Today, Thanksgiving is a true
national holiday. All over the United States,
we travel to celebrate with our families.
It is the biggest travel day of the year.
We travel miles and miles to be with our
grandparents, aunts, uncles, and cousins.
We drive, fly, take the train or the bus.

A father and daughter arrive at the Los Angeles, California, airport in time for Thanksgiving.

We cook
and prepare.

v *Members of a family in Seattle, Washington, check the Thanksgiving gravy.*

For days we cook and prepare the dinner. On Thanksgiving day we cover our tables with a cornucopia of foods. We eat turkey with stuffing. We eat cranberry sauce, cornbread, and mashed potatoes. For dessert we have pies—pumpkin, sweet potato, apple, pecan.

∧ *Miriam Demaris takes a bite of pumpkin pie at her school Thanksgiving feast in Wheeling, West Virginia.*

> *Pumpkin, apple, and pecan pies baked for Thanksgiving.*

Some of our families have come from other countries. We add our own special flavors and foods to the feast. Most of us still have turkey, but when we make stuffing we use flavors and spices from our countries. And with our turkey we eat spring rolls, curry, black beans and rice, and pasta.

∧ A woman prepares a Thanksgiving meal with Mexican flavor for new Latino immigrants in Los Angeles, California.

< In San Antonio, Texas, Rani Pemmaraju and Kalpana Rjagopal serve a Thanksgiving meal that includes traditional dishes from India.

We add our own special flavors.

v In Jacksonville, Florida,
a family enjoys
Thanksgiving dinner.

We say a blessing.

For some of us, Thanksgiving is a religious day. Back in the time of the Pilgrims, there were harvest festivals and there were separate religious days of thanksgiving. Those days were solemn ones filled with prayer and fasting—not feasting. Today we combine the two. We pray at special services. Then we come home to feast! We say a blessing before our meal.

< *The Caedenas family prays after an interfaith Thanksgiving service in San Antonio, Texas.*

∧ *In San Francisco, California, volunteers serve 7,000 Thanksgiving meals to homeless and poor people.*

Thanksgiving is a time to

think of others who have less than we do. We invite people to share our Thanksgiving meals. We serve food at soup kitchens. We collect food for the poor. We share our bounty. We also feed our soldiers who are fighting in wars away from home.

> *Marie Schmidgall serves Thanksgiving meals to Verlee Millspaugh and Mabel Pearsall at the annual Community Thanksgiving Dinner in Burlington, Iowa.*

We share our bounty.

< *Petty Officer 3rd Class James Vanderlois (left) and Seaman Eduardo Rivera celebrate Thanksgiving while serving in the Iraq war.*

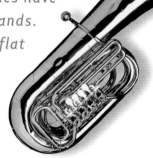

> Many parades have marching bands. This is a b-flat tuba.

∨ Emily Kinder and her cousin James Abla play football after their Thanksgiving feast in Salina, Kansas.

We have other Thanksgiving

traditions. We watch parades. Parades have been part of Thanksgiving since the 1800s. In New York City, the Macy's Thanksgiving Day Parade marks the day with marching bands, floats, and huge, fun balloons.

We also watch football. All over the country, sports fans celebrate by playing and watching football. The tradition of playing sports comes from old harvest festivals, like the one in Plymouth in 1621.

We watch parades and football.

< Bart Simpson flies high on his skateboard at the Macy's Thanksgiving Day Parade in New York City.

23

At the end of

Thanksgiving day we feel
full. We feel full of thanks,
we feel full of family, we
feel full of blessings. And
we feel full of food!

We feel full!

> In Burlington, Iowa, Kaviyaah
Morgan offers his friend Lakendra
Applegate his pumpkin pie at
their school Thanksgiving meal.

For Henry Miller Brotman, born November 20, 2005

PICTURE CREDITS

Pages 1, 4 (top), 6 (bottom), 7: © Sissie Brimberg and Cotton Coulson; Page 2-3: © Scott Sinklier/ Corbis; Page 3(right): © Joe McDonald/Corbis; Page 4 (bottom): © Photodisc/Getty Images; Page 5: © Kimberly Ryan/ The News Sun/ Associated Press; Page 6 (top): © Mark Gormus/ Richmond Times Dispatch/ Associated Press; Page 8: © Neal Hamberg/ Associated Press; Page 9 © Robik Loznak/ Daily Inter Lake/ Associated Press; Page 10: Library of Congress; Page 11: © Trippett/SIPA Press; Page 12-13: © David McNew/ Getty Images; Page 14, 15 (bottom): © Ryan McVay/ Getty Images; Page 15 (top): © Scott McCloskey/ The Wheeling Intelligencer/ Associated Press; page 16 (top): ©Armondo Arorizo/ ZUMA Press; Page 16 (bottom): © BM Sobhani/ San Antonio Express/ ZUMA Press; Page 17: © Kwame Zikomo/ SuperStock; Page 18-19: © Nicol Fruge/ San Antonio Express/ ZUMA Press; Page 20: © Julie Jacobson/ Associated Press; Page 21 (top), 24-25: ©John Lovretta/ The Hawk Eye/ Associated Press; Page 21 (bottom): ©SSgt. Demetrio J. Espinosa/ DOD/ ZUMA Press; 22 (top): © Photodisc/Getty Images; Page 22 (bottom): © Ryan Soderlin/ Salina Journal/ Associates Press; Page 23: © Joseph Sohm/ Corbis; Page 27: University of Texas; page 28: © Lori Epstein; page 29: © Dipak/Reuters/Corbis; Front cover: © Bernd Obermann/ Corbis; Back cover: © Ryan McVay/ Getty Images; Spine: © Chris Stephens/ The Plain Dealer/ Associated Press.

Text copyright © 2006 Deborah Heiligman

Library of Congress Cataloging-in-Publication Data
Heiligman, Deborah.
  Celebrate Thanksgiving / Deborah Heiligman ; consultant, Elizabeth Pleck.
    p. cm. — (Holidays around the world)
  ISBN 0-7922-5928-9 (hardcover) — ISBN 0-7922-5929-7 (lib. bdg.)
  1. Thanksgiving Day—Juvenile literature. 2. Thanksgiving Day—History—Juvenile literature. I. Pleck, Elizabeth Hafkin. II. Title. III. Series: Holidays around the world (National Geographic Society (U.S.))
  GT4975.H44 2006   394.2649—dc22   2006008685

ISBN-10: 0-7922-5928-9 (trade)
ISBN-13: 978-0-7922-5928-2 (trade)
ISBN-10: 0-7922-5929-7 (library)
ISBN-13: 978-0-7922-5929-9 (library)

Book design is by 3+Co.
The body text is set in Mrs. Eaves. The display text is in Lisboa.

FRONT COVER: At the 2003 Macy's Thanksgiving Parade in New York City, a giant inflated turkey promenades down Central Park West. BACK COVER: A girl watches as a nattily dressed young fellow gets ready to stick his finger into a pumpkin pie. TITLE PAGE: A boy enjoys the Thanksgiving feast during a reenactment at Plimoth Plantation.

One of the world's largest nonprofit scientific and educational organizations, the National Geographic Society was founded in 1888 "for the increase and diffusion of geographic knowledge." Fulfilling this mission, the Society educates and inspires millions every day through its magazines, books, television programs, videos, maps and atlases, research grants, the National Geographic Bee, teacher workshops, and innovative classroom materials. The Society is supported through membership dues, charitable gifts, and income from the sale of its educational products. This support is vital to National Geographic's mission to increase global understanding and promote conservation of our planet through exploration, research, and education.

For more information, please call 1-800-NGS-LINE (647-5463) or write to the following address:
NATIONAL GEOGRAPHIC SOCIETY
1145 17th Street N.W., Washington, D.C. 20036-4688 U.S.A.
Visit the Society's Web site at www.nationalgeographic.com

ACKNOWLEDGMENTS

For research help, many thanks to: Lari Robling, author of *Endangered Recipes: Too Good to Be Forgotten*; Valerie Vargas, who shared the Native American prayer with me; Benjamin Weiner, even though his research didn't make the final book; and Laurie Anderson, for a very helpful phone call. Thanks to the good people at the Bank Street Bookstore, who always have the right books. Thanks to Phil and Essie Goldsmith for always hosting wonderful Thanksgivings, and to my whole family for making them warm and fun. A grateful grin to the November 26 birthdays—Jon and Aaron—and to Mom, whose spirit still presides over the day. A special thanks to Laurie Miller Brotman (CL), whose timing made me finish my first draft.